"But seek

a

A Pathway to God's Financial Promises and Peace

TIM ROSEN

Financial Advisor and Founder of Faith and Finance Ministries

All Scripture quotations are taken from the King James Version. Special emphasis in verses is added.

The author and publication team have put forth every effort to give proper credit to quotes and thoughts that are not original with the author. It is not our intent to claim originality with any quote or thought that could not readily be tied to an original source.

ISBN 978-0-98299003-2
Printed in the United States of America

CONTENTS

INTRODUCTION

There has to be an appeal for a reader to buy a book about personal finances. Many times, it is an appeal to get rich, or to learn the "secrets" of millionaires. What is often lacking is biblical teaching aimed at our beliefs.

In our culture, there is a strong, persistent push for more, for success, and for financial independence. Are these pursuits even attainable? Are they measurable? More importantly will God be honored in your quest for either of these?

The answer lies in the heart. The heart desires more, but more than what? More than whom? God knows If we have a legitimate need for more money for the necessities of life. He will work in our lives according to our faith and trust in Him and according to His promises (Matthew 6:33). However, if we believe we will only be happy once we have more—we deceive ourselves. God's Word declares the truth that "He that loveth silver shall not be satisfied with silver, nor he that loveth abundance with increase: this also is vanity." (Ecclesiastes 5:10).

As children of God and Joint Heirs with Jesus we have a greater calling than the pursuits of the world; we have greater rewards and the power of Almighty God to do His will with the finances He entrusts to us. We are not limited in the same ways as the world. For example, the world would say that if you gave money to your church—you would have less—so how will you pay your bills? God says "Honor me with tithes and offerings—and I will more than meet your needs!" (Proverbs 11:24–25 paraphrased).

In the handling of money, we need to guard our hearts. There are many temptations, and with them—many traps and destructive hurts (1 Timothy 6:9). We handle money according to our deep-seated beliefs. We can learn processes, but we will ultimately revert back to habits which were formed by our beliefs. If we can examine and then change our personal beliefs about money, then we can change our outcome. There are many step-by-step programs for financial improvement, but unless our personal beliefs are identified and changed to line up with scriptural truths, we are not likely to experience long term success.

The good news is that God has a path for your finances. In His Word are many precious promises; promises of provision, protection, and even prosperity (beyond material). Where do we find this path? And do we even want this path compared to our own? We can be sure that God's ways are so much better than our own ways (Isaiah 55:8–9).

This path is found in the timeless principles taught in the Bible. In this book I have outlined these principles in steps. I believe there is an order to these principles as one builds upon the other. It is my hope that you would learn these Bible Steps and let God's Word direct your paths before pursuing other financial goals.

BIBLE STEP 1

Depend Completely on God

"Trust in the LORD with all thine heart; and lean not unto thine own understanding."
—PROVERBS 3:5

In our toddler years, we quickly develop trust and dependence upon our parents. This dependence generally remains until our teen years when we cannot wait for our independence. When we enter adulthood, we begin the mindset and behavior (to your parents' relief) of independence. With many years of self-sufficiency under our belt it is not an easy transition back to dependency. Many Christians resist full dependence on God. Just as resisting the dependence upon parents is not in the toddler's best interest, so too is our resistance to dependence on God is not in our best interest. It has always been God's design that His children be completely dependent upon Him alone, so that we would trust Him and witness His power to provide for us and protect us, beyond our own understanding. It is important to realize that our flesh resists, as we prefer to operate by sight—especially in the area of money.

Knowing that we would resist, God instituted a system that would train us in dependence on Him and strengthen our faith. Before we explore this system, please ask yourself a couple of questions:

"Do I believe God's Word?"

"Do I believe that God will do what He says He will do in His Word?"

"Do I believe He has the power to keep His promises?"

"Do I trust Him?"

The Christian life requires faith, and nothing is more rewarding than living fully by faith in our Savior. Are you ready to see God do great things in and through your life, beginning in your heart?

Disclaimer: *The remaining Bible steps will not work for you with any longevity without step one. You must depend on God. There is no shortcut.*

Demonstrate Dependence

Deuteronomy 14:23 says, "…the tithe of thy corn, of thy wine, and of thine oil, and the firstlings of thy herds and of thy flocks; that thou mayest learn to fear the Lord thy God always."

God's system for teaching us to depend completely upon Him is the tithe. His Word teaches us to return to Him a tenth of all of the income He provides to us. Please note, God is not in need of our money – He is not sitting up in heaven wringing His hands waiting on us to tithe. We are the ones in need, and that need is to grow stronger in faith. The system to do so is the tithe. This requires that we trust Him to provide for us, meeting our needs with the remaining ninety percent. Is God able to do that? He most certainly is. Ephesians 3:20 states, "Now into him that is able to do exceeding abundantly above all that we ask or think according to the power that worketh in us."

Living off of ninety percent of our earnings may seem like a form of suffering for Jesus, but God's Word can assure you it is just the opposite. Why would God insist that we live on less money than we earned? So that we can witness Him do the impossible and provide for us beyond our understanding. When He does provide for us, our faith is strengthened. When we honor the Lord by faith, we will see Him keep His promises.

> *"Honor the* Lord *with thy substance and with the firstfruits of all thine increase: So shall thy barns be filled with plenty, and thy presses shall burst out with new wine"*—Proverbs 3:9–10

Notice the phrases *filled with plenty* and *burst out*—these speak of abundance, more than meeting your basic needs. You can safely trust your tithe with God, the one who is "able to do exceeding abundantly above all that we ask or think."

Demonstrate dependence upon Him by trusting Him with the firstfruits of your income.

BIBLE STEP 2

Faithfully Labor

"For even when we were with you, this we commanded you, that if any would not work, neither should he eat."
—2 THESSALONIANS 3:10

God designed us to labor. From the very beginning of mankind, we see God's directive to work so that we may eat: "And God blessed them, and God said unto them, Be fruitful, and multiply, and replenish the earth, and subdue it: and have dominion over the fish of the sea, and over the fowl of the air, and over every living thing that moveth upon the earth" (Genesis 1:28).

Recently, younger lawmakers in our nation's capital, appealing to young voters and "the poor", have begun promoting the belief that labor is oppressive and people should boycott jobs.[1] This is not only troubling to society and the economy but it is also troubling spiritually and goes against God's design.

When we work, we are honoring our Maker and Creator, and we receive the reward for our labor.

> *"For thou shall eat the labor of thine hands: happy shall thou be and it shall be well with thee."*
> —Psalm 128:2

We are able to work because it is God who gives us our abilities. Our skills, know-how, and even the ability to learn a craft or trade all come from the Lord.

> *"But thou shalt remember the Lord thy God: for it is he that giveth thee power to get wealth."*
> —Deuteronomy 8:18.

Whatever work the Lord provides, He wants us to do well—to do the work as if He were our Employer.

---

1 https://townhall.com/tipsheet/bethbaumann/2019/03/10/shes-delusional-aoc-thinks-people-having-to-work-is-a-real-problem-n2542894 (December 1, 2020)

> *"And whatsoever you do, do it heartily, as to the Lord, and not unto men; knowing of that of the Lord you shall receive the reward of inheritance: for you serve the Lord Christ."*
> —COLOSSIANS 3:23–24

Our work ethic should be a God-honoring testimony to those around us. We will not always be treated kindly or even fairly in the work place, especially as we live out our Christian values in the work place, but we are there to please God and not man.

> *"Do all things without murmurings and disputings; That ye may be blameless and harmless, the sons of God, without rebuke, in the midst of a crooked and perverse nation,* ***among whom ye shine as lights in the world;***"—PHILIPPIANS 2:14–15

We should strive to increase the value of our efforts in the eyes of our employer; and it is certainly acceptable to strive for higher earnings when the quality of our work justifies it. When the Lord increases our pay, we can do more to further the kingdom, as well as have more to save for the needs of our families.

> "We must do worldly jobs, but if we do them with sanctified minds, they become offerings to God."
> **—A.W. Tozer**

BIBLE STEP 3

Save a Portion

"He that gathereth in summer is a wise son: but he that sleepeth in harvest is a son that causeth shame."
—PROVERBS 10:5

Americans have no problem spending their income. There are plenty of products and services we want and need. According to the Bureau of Labor Statistics (BLS) 2016 Consumer Expenditure Survey, the average American household spends more than ninety percent of their income.

This does not include interest paid on consumer debt like credit cards. Another troubling statistic is that the average American household cannot handle an unplanned expense of $400.

It's helpful to know that the Bible teaches that spending *all* of our money is foolish (your mom probably told you that is well) and that it is wise to save. "There is treasure to be desired and oil in the dwelling of the wise but a foolish man spendeth it up" (Proverbs 21:20).

You don't have to spend it all.

You don't have to give it all away.

Why is it wise to save?

Expenses, as well as God-honoring opportunities, arise in our lives, and if we have not saved, we will miss those opportunities, and most likely will go into debt in order to handle the unplanned expense.

Many Christians have not been in the habit of saving on a regular basis and may view it as either boring, or impossible, or both. The good news is that it is not difficult to begin saving or, for some, to increase your regular contributions to savings. Let technology do the work for you. Identify a dollar amount that fits in your budget and set up automatic monthly deposits into your savings account, from your checking account. If your bank does not offer this feature, it is really easy to open a savings account with an online bank and set up regular transfers from your other bank account (checking perhaps) into the new savings account, with the frequency of your choice (bi-weekly to stay in line with payday, or monthly).

One of the benefits of automatically saving each month is that you do not have to think about it. If we had to rely on our memory, many of us would simply forget to make a deposit into our savings. You may be surprised to see just how quickly your savings can grow when you make it *automatic.*

BIBLE STEP 4

Giving

"Honour the LORD with thy substance, and with the firstfruits of all thine increase:"
—PROVERBS 3:9

You might expect a book about finances to teach you how to make more, keep more, and multiply your money. On the surface, "Giving" seems on the surface to be the opposite of those actions. But it is just like God to go against man's wisdom and man's ways. He even advised us of that fact back in the book of Isaiah: "For my thoughts are not your thoughts, neither are your ways my ways, saith the Lord. For as the heavens are higher than the earth, so are my ways higher than your ways, and my thoughts than your thoughts" (Isaiah 55:8–9).

So, how is giving supposed to help our finances? Believe it or not, God's financial promises are built around our giving. Promising blessings and provision, He uses giving to train our hearts to part with a portion of that which we love in order to give it to Whom we love. The Bible still promises, "Give, and it shall be given unto you…" (Luke 6:38), and "Honour the LORD with thy substance, and with the firstfruits of all thine increase: So shall thy barns be filled with plenty, and thy presses shall burst out with new wine" (Proverbs 3:9–10). Notice the directive to give first, then His promise is received: "Give, and it shall be given", "Honour the LORD with thy substance…. so shall thy barns be filled with plenty.." This act of worship (giving) requires faith, and God rewards our faith!

There is no money in heaven. Neither is there any worrying, fretting, coveting, idolatry, nor stealing (Can I get an "Amen"?). While we are sojourning here on earth, we have the opportunity to convert today's money into treasure, forever to be enjoyed in heaven. Jesus teaches us in Matthew 6:21, "But lay up for **yourselves treasure** in heaven, where neither moth nor rust doth corrupt, and where thieves do not break through nor steal" (emphasis added). Jesus is not being metaphorical here, but literal. As we give to the Lord, in this present life, He stores that gift for us as literal treasure in heaven to be enjoyed and shared in fellowship forever. This act of parting with something we value trains us to have a heart for eternity. In the very next verse Jesus says, "For where your treasure is, there will your heart be also" (verse 21). God does not want our hearts fixed on the things of this world, which will perish (1 John 2:15–17); He wants our hearts set on and desiring the "...things which are above, where Christ sitteth on the right hand of God" (Colosians 3:1).

BIBLE STEP 5

Live within Your Means

"Be thou diligent to know the state of thy flocks,
and look well to thy herds."
—PROVERBS 27:23

King Solomon asked of God to have wisdom. In response to his request, God gave Solomon more wisdom than any other person, along with great wealth. Through this wisdom from God, Solomon ruled and reigned over Israel and wrote most of the book of Proverbs as well as two other books of the Bible. He wrote much on the subject of wealth (he was very qualified).

In Proverbs 27:23, he wrote, "Be thou diligent to know the state of thy flocks, and look well to thy herds." How easy is it to simply keep on reading past this verse without catching its meaning? After all, I do not have flocks or herds, do you?

When we understand that from the time of this writing, through the nineteenth century in America, most families farmed for a living, so they were well acquainted with agricultural terms. One's flocks and herds well represented his wealth. Today, in the absence of measuring our wealth with livestock, we can apply this passage as *Be diligent to know the state of your money, and look well to your bank accounts.* As stewards of the resources entrusted to us by God, we are expected to be diligent to know where our dollars are going. You do not need to be taught on how easy it is to spend money in today's culture. The challenge seems to be in the refraining from spending, whether that translates to actual shopping, or taking on monthly bills that end up choking our financial health.

God set His own children apart from the "heathen" to be a testimony of God's power and provision. The Old Testament is full of instructions on how the Jews ought to live.

As His children today, the wisdom still applies. God does not want His children burdened down in debt, which is a form of bondage (Proverbs 22:7), He wants us to be generous to those in need (Proverbs 3:27 28), and to be honest in our financial dealings (Proverbs 11:1). When we live within our income, we are able to pay our obligations on time, avoid debt, and maintain a godly testimony to the world around us. It is difficult to share the gospel to someone we have borrowed from, or even worse, someone to whom we are indebted. Keeping a godly testimony allows for more open doors to present the Gospel of Christ.

Knowing the consequences of not living within our means, in advance, may serve as motivation. Who wants to sign up for stress, frustration, fear, the sense of being in bondage, the avoidance of many loved ones, or the need to say "no" constantly to wonderful opportunities?

BIBLE STEP 6

Avoid Consumer Debt

"The rich ruleth over the poor, and the borrower is servant to the lender."
—PROVERBS 22:7

It's no secret that the world promotes and celebrates immorality. With every passing year, behaviors which the world declares to be socially acceptable get worse and worse. As Christians, we need to remain diligent in guarding our hearts against the world's constant pushing of how we should live, what we should look like, what we should buy, and how we should be entertained.

While we should be well aware of the blatant sins which the world accepts (fornication, covetousness, greed, lying, and theft), it's the subtle appeals to our flesh that most often ensnare us. It seems normal to watch commercials with the messages of: "Visa. Everywhere you want to be," "American Express: Don't live life without it," "There are some things money can't buy. For everything else, there's Mastercard," or "It pays to Discover."

Have you noticed how easy it is to buy something you want with a credit card? Have you experienced how difficult it is, sometimes, to pay off the bill for that purchase? I am reminded of calories. It is so tempting, so easy, to consume those extra, delicious calories (who's counting anyway, right?) yet so hard, yea impossible it may seem, to burn off those calories!

Americans as a group have no problem saying yes to purchasing on credit, and saying no to paying the bill in full—resulting in carrying debt. When we retain a debt balance, we end up sending our wealth to a faceless bank— instead of building our own financiall health. To illustrate, let's say that your car needs repair work, and the total bill comes to $1,400. In the case where you do not have money saved up in the bank, you "pay" for it with a credit card. Next month, when you receive your credit card bill, you see that your "Minimum payment" is only $27. Whew! What a relief, you tell yourself. I can handle $27. The bank (the Lender) is charging 27% interest, but they have you focused on the "reduction to the ridiculous"—a small, manageable payment of only $27. At that pace, it will take eleven years to pay off your balance, and you will have paid that bank $4,278!

Let that sink in, you paid triple the original cost of your car repair which translates to a profit of $2,878 to the bank. Let's pause and ask, "Did any of your savings accounts earn $2,878 in that same period?" Likely not.

This is a very realistic example, as the average American household carries a lot more than $1,400 in credit card debt; the balance is closer to $15,482. Imagine paying $258 per month to a bank that does not love you, does not love your children, and will do nothing to help you when you experience a financial crisis.

Obviously, it is wiser to pay yourself that $258 and build your financial health instead of the lender's. The wisdom of Solomon seems crystal clear as he wrote, "The rich ruleth over the poor, and the borrower is servant to the lender." (Proverbs 22:7). The reference to "servant" actually means indentured servitude—this individual is in bondage until the debt is completely paid off. God does not want His children in bondage, and this type of bondage is self-inflicted—we can avoid it and live free. This happens when we discipline ourselves to say no to the immediate want, and yes to saving and paying ourselves (Bible Step Three).

BIBLE STEP 7

Save for Major Purchases

"The thoughts of the diligent tend only to plenteousness; but of every one that is hasty only to want."
—PROVERBS 21:10

If something is worth having, it is worth saving and waiting for (now I'm sounding like a parent, right?). Saving and waiting have their benefits. When we take *time* to save up for an intended purchase, it helps us avoid *impulse* buying. Impulse purchases are usually made hastily, and without much consideration as to whether it is a wise, or even needed, purchase. Impulse purchases are most-often regretted.

Waiting also allows for consideration as to whether it is God's will that such a purchase is made. We are called to be faithful stewards of God's resources. This does not mean that we cannot have nice things, it does mean that we should wait and know if we have a peace about such a large purchase before "striking hands" and committing to it.

Most of us can recall a time when we "bit off more than we could chew"—we spent more money than we should have on an item such as a wide screen TV, a piece of jewelry, or maybe a new car. Sure, we enjoyed the new item for a while (or enjoyed the act of giving to someone else), but soon after, we experienced the impact of spending too much, getting behind on other bills, incurring late fees, having purchases repossessed. This impact also includes stress, arguments, the absence of discretionary dollars, and sadly in some cases—divorce.

> *"For which of you, intending to build a tower, sitteth not down first, and counteth the cost, whether he have sufficient to finish it? Lest haply, after he hath laid the foundation, and is not able to finish it, all that behold it begin to mock him,*

Saying, This man began to build, and was not able to finish.”—Luke 14:28

BIBLE STEP 8

Be Slow to Take on Monthly Bills

"Be not thou one of them that strike hands, or of them that are sureties for debts."
—PROVERBS 22:26

In today's economy, the majority of financial transactions are processed digitally. There are digital agreements, digital signatures, and the digital transferring of dollars. Many times, cash is not even handled.

Not too long ago, agreements were made, and commitments were sealed with a handshake. The expression "Let's shake on it" is not far removed from recent memory. Scripture uses a similar term to picture the act of taking on a commitment, or an obligation (usually financial), striking hands.

Every mention in the Bible of "striking hands," to pledge or mortgage, is negative.

> *"A man void of understanding striketh hands, and becometh surety in the presence of his friend."*
> —Proverbs 17:18

It is easy to take on additional monthly obligations, based on the "low monthly payment of only $....". We sign up for gym memberships, music services, TV, food delivery, car payments, just about anything we can think of—agreeing to pay a monthly fee. When we are not diligent, all these seemingly *little* monthly bills add up and then choke our family finances.

We find ourselves reluctantly saying we "can't afford" to do this or that, or to go here or there, though we may be earning a very nice income. Although recent surveys indicate that the average American household income is $62,175, we *feel* like we are poor, because we are quick to strike hands, and we pile one new monthly obligation upon another.

The solution is to prayerfully consider and budget both the needs and the *wants*. As a budget serves as a God-honoring spending plan, a Christian budget would factor in, and protect, tithes and offerings, and fixed expenses such as housing, transportation, insurance, utilities, and education. Then, we should then carefully decide upon the *variables* such as dining, entertainment, shopping, and personal care.

When we are slow to "strike hands", we keep ourselves from a snare of financial bondage.

BIBLE STEP 9

Trust Him through Trials

"That the trial of your faith, being much more precious than of gold that perisheth, though it be tried with fire, might be found unto praise and honour and glory at the appearing of Jesus Christ: "

—1 PETER 1:7

We all face financial trials in one form or another. When we are in the thick of a trial it is very tempting to try to get out as quickly as possible, often relying on our own methods.

Someone drowning in debt may seek relief through a consolidation loan or worse— borrow from family.

Recently laid off employees may be quick to take the first job that they can get, though it may not be God's will for them to work there. First Peter 1:7

teaches us that the fruit of going through the trial, the strengthening of our faith, is actually more valuable than the money we are struggling over. When we respond by faith in the midst of a trial, that faith is strengthened, and we are then more equipped to be used mightily of the Lord.

The Lord knows our needs, and He is our provider. Frustration and fear occur when we set expectations of how we wanted the trial to be resolved but it does not happen our way or in our timeline. Still, God is good and His ways are higher than ours.

Seek Him, especially in the trial and know that He will provide: "But seek ye first the kingdom of God and his righteousness and all these things shall be added unto you" (Matthew 6:33).

Continue to honor him with your income during the trial, and watch Him meet your needs beyond your understanding:

> *"Honour the Lord with thy substance, and with the first fruits of all the thine increase: So shall thy*

barns be filled with plenty, and thy presses shall burst out with new wine."

—Proverbs 3:9-10

BIBLE STEP 10

A Second Chance

"And the lord commended the unjust steward, because he had done wisely."—LUKE 16:8

"There will be a day when each and every child of God will stand before Him and give an account for his stewardship."—2 CORINTHIANS 5:10

We have all made financial mistakes at some point, some small, some big, and maybe even disastrous. Perhaps even now you may not be where you want to be, financially. Thankfully, God is patient, and desires that we grow in our faith, in our walk with Him, and in our dependence on Him. Peter wrote, in 2 Peter 3:18, "But grow in grace, and in the knowledge of our Lord and Saviour Jesus Christ." To grow is an ongoing process; Peter did not admonish "Be perfect—

now!" but rather, to *grow*. That means that mistakes will be made, so will unwise decisions, and there may be some reaping from the mistakes sown—but we can *grow*. We can and should learn from those mistakes while learn the biblical principles of money and work to apply them to our lives.

In the sixteenth chapter of Luke's gospel, we read a parable which is commonly known as "The parable of the unjust steward," yet the Bible records that this *unjust* steward is commended by his employer. How is it that someone who apparently was crooked and unfaithful with his employer's finances, and in the process of being fired, ends up being commended?

The answers lie in this man's choices and actions *after* being informed that he would be fired.

> *"Then the steward said within himself, What shall I do? for my lord taketh away from me the stewardship: I cannot dig; to beg I am ashamed. I am resolved what to do, that, when I am put out of the stewardship, they may receive me into their houses. So he called every one of his lord's debtors unto him, and said unto the first, How much owest*

> *thou unto my lord? And he said, An hundred measures of oil. And he said unto him, Take thy bill, and sit down quickly, and write fifty. Then said he to another, And how much owest thou? And he said, An hundred measures of wheat. And he said unto him, Take thy bill, and write fourscore."*
> —LUKE 16:3-7

While we do not know the details of how poorly he previously managed his employer's financial affairs, we do know that he had an abrupt "wake-up call" and quickly turned 180 degrees in his work ethic. Rather than being slothful, he jumped into action and conducted business shrewdly, giving a discount to some customers, and bringing in some cash to his boss. Reportedly, the results of his efforts so pleased his lord that he is commended: "And the lord commended the unjust steward, because he had done wisely" (verse 8).

There are many practical applications from this parable of a man who became suddenly aware of the consequences of his poor financial stewardship and took corrective action. We will be rewarded for our faithfulness (1 Corinthians 3:14), and we stand to lose rewards for the areas in which we were unfaithful (1 Corinthians 3:15). Knowing this now, we should then have an urgency to be faithful stewards today. How we have handled money in the past is the past. Please don't wait for a wake-up call, like the unjust steward received. Today we can and should choose to honor the Lord with the finances He has provided and seek to grow in this area—financial stewardship. This is our second chance.

CONCLUSION

We all have our own individual and specific beliefs about money. Throughout our childhood and early adulthood, we create beliefs, thoughts, attitudes, and assumptions about money that heavily influence many of the financial decisions we make throughout our lives. We have had years, even decades, of handling money our way, and we reap what we sow. We can trust God and believe that His ways are truly higher than our ways.

These Bible Steps may not be easy, but neither is living a daily sanctified life; yet all are possible when we yield our will to the Lord and trust His process. You may not master each principle right away, but hang in there. Praise God, He is patient and allows us to grow in grace. I encourage you to study and pray about one step at time, asking God for understanding and guidance in each one. When we follow His ways, we do receive His promises, power and peace!

Made in the USA
Columbia, SC
09 February 2025

53107751R00033